Virtues and Values

FACETS

Selected Titles in the Facets Series

Virtues and Values
The African and African American Experience

Peter J. Paris

Fortress Press
Minneapolis

VIRTUES AND VALUES
The African and African American Experience

Cover art: *Continuity* by James Noel. Used by permission of the artist.

ISBN 0-8006-3661-9

The paper used in this publication meets the minimum requirements of American National Standard for Information Sciences — Permanence of Paper for Printed Library Materials, ANSI Z329.48-1984.

Manufactured in the U.S.A.

Contents

Preface

Some years ago I wrote a book titled *The Spirituality of African Peoples: The Search for a Common Moral Discourse.* That book was inspired by the experience of being an African Canadian working in Nigeria four decades ago and subsequently emigrating to the United States, where I am now a naturalized American citizen.

Throughout those wanderings, the shadow of the African slave trade has never been far from my consciousness. My first sight of Africa filled me with tears, as I thought about my ancestors who had been stolen from their villages, imprisoned in the dungeons at Elmina, Goree Island, or elsewhere, and pressed onto ships that transported their shackled bodies to a new world of untold suffering. Ironically, their longing to return to their homeland would not be fulfilled until their descendants freely chose to do so in memory of them.

Also, when I first came to live in the United States, I felt a similar sense of return to an ancestral homeland. Following the American Revolutionary War, Africans who had helped the British joined white Loyalists in their emigration to Halifax, Nova Scotia, where they were given the political status of free persons, though racially discriminated against and segregated for the next century and a half. Thus, as an African Canadian, I have good reason to claim two ancestral homelands. My ancestors came from Africa as slaves; they also came from the United States as racial pariahs. I have returned to both places, and I claim each of them as an indelible part of my heritage.

As I reflect on the meaning of being African on the continent and elsewhere in the diaspora, I have striven to grasp the connecting threads of those varied experiences. Apart from the sphere of genetics, I have asked myself the following question: "What is the enduring African factor that is recognizable by African peoples everywhere?" In other words, is there an African value or virtue that can be expressed in different cultural and linguistic forms? Such a discovery would render the word *African* meaningful whenever it is used adjectivally to designate peoples as African American, African Canadian, and so forth. In opposition to E. Franklin Frazier's claim that the African past had been totally obliterated under the conditions of slavery, the anthropologist Melville Herskovits provided some hard evidence in support of the alternative argument that some African practices did in fact survive that bitter experience.

In *The Spirituality of African Peoples,* I argue that Africans did not come to these shores as a *tabula rasa.* Rather, they brought their religious, moral, and aesthetic values with them, and throughout that horrific period they preserved those values in various ways. But the preservation did not occur in any pure form. As a result of their interactions with the American environment, their African worldviews were gradually shaped into a new African consciousness. Gradually, a hybrid of African and American elements combined to form the nucleus of what we now call the African American culture. Thus I contend that the experiences of African peoples in America and throughout the diaspora cannot be fully understood apart from their continuities with the cultural ethos of the African homeland. Identifying the African factor in the African American experience was the goal of that project. Since hard empirical evidence in support of that claim was not possible, a plausible argument in support of my claim was sufficient.

Clearly, there are those who argue that the immense diversity of peoples and cultures on the African continent prevent us from discerning any such commonality among them. Let me hasten to say, however, that while I readily acknowledge the diversity of African peoples, I contend nonetheless that a dynamic principle of unity permeates that diversity and provides the basis for African identity. Analogously, as the western world is comprised of many diverse peoples and cultures, we can speak nonetheless of a western identity. Similarly, many Pan-Africanists long ago persuaded African peoples everywhere to affirm their common identity and to unite in a common cause for freedom and justice.

Thus, this small book is an extract from the larger book, in which I argued that the traditions of African peoples are diverse in form though united in their underlying spirituality. Accordingly, I provided an analysis of the broad consensus among African peoples that the three forms of life, namely, nature, history, and spirit, are ontologically united and hence interdependent. That work culminated in a discussion of a common set of moral virtues that are highly valued by African peoples everywhere. Those virtues are grounded in an African cosmology that is the foundation for all African theologies and ethics. That concluding discussion comprises the content of *Virtues and Values*. I hope that those who read this book will be motivated to investigate the subject more deeply in its parental volume.

1

The African Factor in the African American Experience

Africans and African Americans share a common worldview, which comprises a cosmological whole and unites all of life in and among the realms of spirit, history, and nature. African spirituality—the dynamic and integrating power that constitutes the principal frame of reference for all individual and collective experiences—has been preserved in recognizable form among the North American diaspora. This does not mean that it has been preserved exactly as it had been several centuries ago in Africa. Rather, since all living traditions necessarily change over time, African traditions not only adapted themselves to their new environment but also altered it in many important ways. Thus, basic African religious and moral values were preserved in western cultural forms. The result has been the gradual emergence of an African American culture that contains an amalgam of African and American elements.

The basic building blocks for an African and African American social ethic are derived from and reflective of the dynamic structural unity among the four constitutive spheres of African experience, namely: God, community, family, person. Furthermore, those four spheres of experience are fully interdependent. No single sphere can flourish apart from all the others. Their interdependence is manifested in a variety of reciprocal functions, much like the interrelations among the parts of a living organism.

Similarly, the interdependence of individuals and the community has major implications for all human activities. For instance, since individuals are part of the community, the latter must assume responsibility for both the good and the bad actions of the former. Thus the community celebrates the good that individuals do, and, whenever their bad actions offend either some divinity or an ancestor, the community must repent of those actions by offering propitiatory sacrifices to counteract the ill effects of the deed.[1] Africans never view wrongdoing as strictly an individual matter.

Many African traditions have undergone changes in the diaspora. African slaves utilized various European cultural forms for the transmission of African values. They wove various African meanings into those new cultural forms through creative processes of improvisation, practices that Henry Louis Gates has defined as analogous to the African and African American vernacular traditions of *signifying*.[2] Admittedly, the means by which African values were transmitted to the so-called new world differed in accordance with the conditions of slavery. For example, in those areas where African slaves far outnumbered their captors and had minimal face-to-face contact with them, many African traditions were easily preserved with little modification. Numerous examples of these are extant in various parts of the Caribbean Islands and most prominently in Brazil. In other areas, however, and especially in the United States, where they were rigorously controlled and stringently forbidden to continue African customs, slaves were forced to conceal the latter from their owners by camouflaging them in cultural forms that usually conveyed double meanings, one for the eyes and ears of slaveowners, the other for slaves.

2

Virtue Theory

The preservation and promotion of community is the paramount goal of African peoples in all spheres of life. It is a practical goal deeply rooted in their cosmological thought and constitutive of all personal and public life.[1] Thus, it is not only descriptive of public reality but also normative for every part of it. In other words, it is the determinative measure of value for all human activities. In fact, the purpose of all the realms of life (spirit, history, and nature) is to preserve and promote the well-being of the community, the breadth of which varies in accordance with the nature of particular political alliances between and among various tribal groups. In the descending order of power from the supreme God, through the subdivinities, ancestral spirits, communal and familial leaders, to the youngest child, the highest good of each is the same, namely, the preservation and promotion of the community's well-being.

The anthropocentric nature of African cosmological thought and the holism it entails imply a sacramental view of life in general and of human life in particular. Yet African anthropocentrism does not imply either the superiority of humans over other forms of life or a denial of the supremacy of the deity over all existence. Nor does it constitute a rationale justifying wanton exploitation by humans of natural resources. It merely means that humans are at the center of a sacred cosmos in which they are expected to assume immense responsibilities for the preservation of its unity. The integral relationships between humans and invisible superior powers require a reciprocity of functions between them both. In return for their devotion and faithfulness, humans can expect the protection of both the divinities and the ancestors from a variety of unfriendly cosmic forces. In other words, it is the responsibility of humans to take the initiative in maintaining good communal relations with the invisible world of spirits. If they exercise their responsibilities well, they will receive appropriate compensation in the form of a good life. If they fail to do so, they will suffer misfortune. Insofar as humans are faithful in their devotion to the invisible spirits, they can rightly expect reciprocity. Hence, it is common for Africans and African Americans alike (whether they be traditionalists, Christians, or Muslims) to offer prayers in the form of petitions for the basic conditions of life: health, food, shelter, and protection from all forms of evil including social abuse, political oppression, and economic deprivation. In fact, Africans view religious devotion and good moral habits as necessary conditions for the prevention and the solution of most practical problems in daily life. It is virtually inconceivable for Africans to think of human existence apart from its dependent relationship on God, the divinities, and the ancestral spirits. Consequently, there are no atheists among them.

This sacramental view of life does not claim any primordial cosmological fault in the nature of humanity as such. In fact, African cosmologies have nothing comparable to a doctrine of original sin[2] that condemns the whole of humanity. This does not mean that Africans view all humans as morally good. Nothing could be further from the truth, and evidence to the contrary is quite abundant. Rather, in contrast to those who are born with good destinies, it is widely believed that some people are bearers of various types of bad destinies. Some of them are capable of modification; others are not. In either case, with the combined help of professional diviners and much concentrated effort on their own part, humans may to a certain extent overcome many aspects of a bad destiny. Thus the notion of destiny, whether good or bad, does not imply human passivity. Instead it informs persons about the possibilities that they are either capable or incapable of realizing.

Clearly, the holistic worldview of Africans implies a sacramental view of life. Additionally, the practical goal of community as the highest good, coupled with the reciprocal relationships between persons and invisible spirits, signal the pragmatic nature of all African thought in relation to each of the realms of life, namely, spirit, history, and nature. As a matter of fact, Africans are not easily disposed to speculative thought because it tends to have little or no empirical basis. Rather, much of African thought, including that of theology and ethics, arises out of the problems of daily experience, and it is pursued for the purpose of discovering practical solutions for everyday problems. In short, African theology and ethics are practical sciences in the service of the community's well-being. Hence both are intrinsically political.

Having identified the paramount goal of African and African American thought and practice, let us now discuss the necessary capacities and moral attributes needed for its realization. As we will see, both the capacities and the moral attributes have their empirical bases in the worldviews of African peoples. Among African peoples on the continent and in the diaspora good moral character constitutes the nature of the moral life, and it is both rooted in and derived from God, the creator and preserver of all that is.

To advance this argument in as clear and concise a way as possible, I have decided to adopt the following illustrative method. First, I will draw upon the inspirational resources provided by the momentous events in late-twentieth-century South Africa, namely, the inauguration of Nelson Rolihlahla Mandela as the first president of that republic to be elected by universal franchise. The whole world agreed that Mandela is an extraordinary person and a leader *par excellence.* His moral character accounts for both. Certainly there appeared to be no doubt in his mind or in that of his followers that the good for himself and the good for the community were the same, even though the community's realization of its good was greater because its sphere of responsibility included all the people. Evidence of this philosophy permeated all of his speeches. In my judgment, no African embodies that ethic more completely in our day than Nelson Mandela, whose strength of character has inspired countless millions both on the continent and around the world. As my argument unfolds, relevant dimensions of his life and moral development will be explicated.

Second, I will also illustrate this ethic by drawing on the resources of the long struggle of African Americans for citizenship rights in the United States and, more specifically, the moral attributes of Martin Luther King Jr., whose personal integrity and leadership skills have been immortalized not only in the United States but globally. President Mandela and Dr. King are moral exemplars of the African and African American ethic respectively. They share a common spirituality, and their names have become worldwide metaphors for the struggle for the realization of a unified multiracial (in South Africa commonly called "nonracial") community. Interestingly, one discovers very little substantive discussion of African or African American culture in the writings or speeches of either of the two men. Yet the immense impact of their respective cultures on each of them is unmistakable.[3] In my judgment, because of their interest in providing grounds for an expansive community, they saw little need to focus attention on the specificity of their particular cultures. Yet nothing in their respective teachings violates the basic values implicit in their respective African and African American cultures.

The form of the African and African American social ethic I wish to explicate is that of moral virtue (that is, moral excellence), which is deeply rooted in and reflective of a particular spirituality. The basis of this ethic in the common worldview of African and African American peoples separates it significantly from other traditions of virtue ethics that draw their source material from different cultural situations in order to address the moral issues implicit in those contexts.[4]

As in all theories of moral virtue, African and African American virtues are dispositions that are not innate. They are acquired by habitual practices, preferably begun in early childhood through teaching and practice. In turn, they eventually produce certain types of character that dispose persons to do certain kinds of things. Since habits can be either good or bad, their quality is determined by that of the goal they serve. Thus the virtues of African and African American ethics are teleological. That is to say, they are determined by the goal of preserving and promoting community, which we have seen is the ultimate goal of all African peoples. Further and most important, these peoples find their fulfillment in the pursuit of that goal.

Thus African and African American ethics is primarily concerned with the development of a certain kind of moral character, a character that reflects the basic values of their respective communities. Morality pertains to the cultural ethos and hence is culturally specific.[5] According to this perspective, there is no universal morality as such, even though some common moral values are widespread among diverse cultural groups. Yet in my judgment morality is univocal only within particular communities. That is to say, it is determined by the norms, values, and goals of particular communities. The resolution of conflictual relationships between and among communities requires that all concerned be in agreement with the norms, values, and goals of some transcendent community in which the conflicting groups share membership. If they do not share such membership, conflicts among them cannot be resolved apart from the construction of some consensual framework.

In virtue ethics the quality of a person's character determines the quality of that person's actions and vice versa. The circularity of this argument is important because it demonstrates the relation of being and doing. Each implies the other. For example, a person of moral virtue is one who exercises good habits, and, conversely, the exercise of good habits constitutes a person of moral virtue.

An important question that arises in every discussion of virtue ethics is the following: "Why should a person become morally virtuous?" Invariably, the answer to that question is, in a word, *self-realization.* That is, like everything else in the world, a person's life has an ultimate goal, the attainment of which marks the person's full growth. If that ultimate goal is the preservation and promotion of community, as I have argued it is for Africans and African Americans, and if the acquisition of moral virtues is the means to that end, then a person becomes morally virtuous in order to make a substantial contribution to the preservation and promotion of the community. Since the African understanding of community is integrally related to God and the entire realm of spirit, the goal of self-realization is a transcendent goal that is sacramental in nature. Its pursuit is what W. E. B. DuBois once called a "spiritual striving."

The ethics of moral virtue is practical in every sense. Its goal is knowledge of the moral good that humans can do in order to become morally good. Thus, knowing the good is for the sake of doing good and becoming good. In that respect, virtue ethics has much in common with art. Unlike some arts, however, which produce artifacts that lie outside the process of doing, virtue ethics is like music in that its goal is not separate from the practice. As there is no music apart from playing music, there can be no good people apart from the doing of good actions. Good action is always goal-oriented, and its goodness is determined by the extent to which its quality is commensurate with that of the goal it serves. Thus clarity about the goal is the first principle of good action.[6]

Yet practical habits from which moral virtues emerge are not acquired easily. They involve effort and sometimes discomfort. As learning to play a musical instrument is stressful in the beginning, practice eventually renders the activity seemingly easy because it becomes a habit and thus it can be performed without thinking. That is not to say, however, there is no thought in the habit. Rather, the thought is absorbed into the activity.

A distinctive feature of African and African American ethics is its grounding in a cosmological spirituality that unites three interdependent realms of life, which are usually ranked in hierarchical order— spirit, history, and nature. Thus all life is sacred. This is a fundamental principle for all African peoples. Unlike in most western thought, the sacred is not separated from human and natural life but permeates both. As a consequence, the function of human life is a sacred vocation, namely, to preserve and promote the life of the community. That is also the sacred obligation of the entire community and each of its individual members. Further, all the traditions of the community serve that end. Whenever that life-affirming function is thwarted or perverted by some evil force, then appropriate propitiation must be undertaken by the community in compliance with the prevailing wisdom of the elders and diviners. The evil force must be expunged so that the life of the community can continue.

Since the whole of life is sacred and since the moral virtue of individuals and that of the community are the same, African and African American ethics aims at enabling individual persons to become good so that they will also become good leaders in their respective communities. Africans and African Americans cannot conceive of the one apart from the other.

Hence the goal of their ethics is the moral development of both the person and the community.

3

Some African and African American Moral Virtues

Within this framework we note specific virtues that are highly praised by both Africans and African Americans. As we will see, each virtue requires a natural capacity and adequate social conditions that support its development. This does not mean that the virtue is produced by either nature or social conditioning. On the contrary, each virtue is acquired through the long process of proper habituation through teaching and practice. Many African practices, however, are communal, namely, festivals, rituals, and ceremonial rites of passage, all of which are imbued with religious and moral meanings.

Further, each virtue designates both a psychic and communal value. That is to say, each is a value for the individual as well as one for the community. The former connotes personal development; the latter, leadership development. Both are interrelated; the one implies the other. This crucial feature of the African and African American ethic connotes the integral person-community relationship that is basic to the African and African American understanding of each.

Finally, I will try to name the converse of both the moral virtues and their corresponding leadership styles, taking care to illustrate the latter with reference to Nelson Mandela and Dr. King. Let me add, however, that no attempt will be made to be comprehensive in naming all the virtues. In fact, I have no way of knowing how many virtues there may be. Thus, I will name what appear to me to be the most prominent ones.

Beneficence

No virtue is more highly praised among Africans and African Americans than that of beneficence; it exemplifies the goal of community as it is internalized by individual persons and community leaders. That is to say, the individual's disposition is so shaped by the ultimate goal of community that he or she finds contentment in facilitating the well-being of others. For them, the good of others always assumes priority over their own good. During a recent visit to South Africa I decided to telephone my friends in Soweto near the end of the conference I was attending. Knowing that they would inevitably invite me to spend some days with them, I had taken that into consideration in booking my return flight. When they learned, however, that I had been staying in a hotel in Johannesburg for almost a week while attending the conference, they expressed deep sorrow. "That is not the way we treat our friends," my Sowetan host said. In his mind, people stay in hotels only when they have neither family members nor friends in the area. It made no difference to him that transporting me daily to and from the conference would have inconvenienced him and his family. From his point of view, such an inconvenience was the sacrifice he would gladly have made on behalf of his friend, and, further, I should not have been concerned about that matter. Moreover, he felt embarrassed that his friends might learn about this matter and in some way blame him. He tried to impress upon me that, because we are friends, I am his family's responsibility whenever I visit his country, and I should not deny them that pleasure.

During that same trip, I had also arranged to visit a former student who lived a longer distance away from Johannesburg. Upon arriving, to my surprise I discovered that he and his wife had prepared to give me their bedroom and bath for the whole period, while they and another visiting relative slept with their three children. Once again I was deeply concerned about the inconvenience I was causing the family. From their perspective, though, they were honored by my visit, and they welcomed the temporary sacrifice of convenience because of that honor. The whole experience was reminiscent of the many times my own mother and father willingly gave up their bedroom for the comfort of guests, sometimes guests whom they had not known for very long. It was taken for granted throughout my community that guests were to receive the best the family had to offer.

For well over a century the African United Baptist Association of Nova Scotia was hosted annually by their respective member churches throughout the province. In each location where the association met, the entire black community, including those who were not members of the churches, participated in hosting the out-of-town guests by providing meals and lodging in their small homes. Since virtually none had spare guest rooms, family members often slept on the floor in order to accommodate more guests than the house seemed able to hold. In recent years this traditional practice has gradually changed, as growing numbers of delegates can afford to stay in hotels that had been in previous years racially segregated. In spite of the immense amount of work involved by the hosting families, the joy and delight of it all was that the guests should return to their respective homes feeling that they had been treated well. Their turn to reciprocate would eventually come. Such an annual custom corresponds well with the African view of hospitality.

The above examples anecdotally illustrate the virtue of beneficence. The practical adjustments made by all family members in hosting visitors impart to children a good part of their training in the gradual acquisition of the same virtue.

Development of the virtue of beneficence is always well supported by a good destiny. Beneficent people come into the world blessed by God and destined for greatness. In Africa their names become bearers of their destiny pointing to the way in which their lives should develop. Similarly, a good destiny is recognized among those African Americans who are named after family members, prominent heroes, or cherished celebrities. In each case, it is hoped that the children will live up to their good names and fulfill all the expectations of their families.

Being born with a good destiny implies birth into a family of commensurate value that possesses all the necessary resources needed for the child's moral development. Destiny requires basic, supportive familial conditions of physical security, economic viability, and good will: moral development can only occur in a moral context.

Synonyms for beneficence are many. They include hospitality, generosity, liberality, benevolence, magnanimity, love. The beneficent person is a person of good will, one who joyfully extends hospitality to all alike. In this respect the beneficent person respects all persons. Though morally superior to ordinary people, the beneficent person is quite unaware of his or her moral goodness. Like all moral virtues, beneficence functions as a second nature for the one who is beneficent.

Africans and African Americans expect their leaders to be beneficent. That is to say, they expect them to share their bounty with all their people because nothing is more glorious than the communal enjoyment of its wealth. Private acquisition of property in whatever form for the enjoyment of the individual or a small elite is the converse of a beneficent spirit. Further, by not counting the cost, the beneficent person is not controlled primarily by the principle of efficiency.

Former South African President Nelson Mandela embodies the virtue of beneficence. His gracious spirit of good will is abundant, and his magnanimous hospitality to all and especially to his former oppressor is nearly unbelievable. The relationship that developed between him and his warden of twenty years, James Gregory, has seemed equally incredible to the world at large. Yet these and numerous other acts of kindness merely demonstrate the man's beneficent character. Undoubtedly, the source of his moral development was the training he received in three places: (1) the royal family into which he was born; (2) Fort Hare University, the prominent university founded by missionaries in order to give blacks throughout southern Africa access to excellence in higher education, where he was educated; and (3) the African National Congress (ANC), of which he frequently has identified himself as a disciplined member. All of these institutions have embodied the African and African American goal of preserving and promoting community.

In his cultivation of beneficence as a moral virtue, Mandela's character was fully formed long before he was sentenced to prison in his early forties. That spirit continued to express itself throughout those years as he exercised leadership from his prison cell and, eventually, became a worldwide symbol of the underground struggle against apartheid. When he walked out of prison on February 11, 1990, after having served twenty-seven years of a life sentence in pursuit of the rights of citizenship for his people, the world to its astonishment saw and heard a kingly man with a beneficent spirit that was more embracing than most could imagine.

Mandela's beneficent spirit contributed immeasurably to his unmistaken similarity to a traditional African king, who is invariably a statesperson in every sense of the word. Such a leader is good-spirited; dedicates himself wholly to the good of all the people; knows his place in the scheme of things; is a willing servant of the masses; listens carefully to them and knows that ultimate authority rests in those whose needs the leader is charged to serve; is confident of his power; is courageous; is willing to negotiate and compromise with his enemies for the good of the community; always rules wisely in accordance with the desires and needs of the community; and is open to the idea of an expansive community of ever-increasing diversity.

Martin Luther King Jr. represented African America's most prominent embodiment of the virtue of beneficence. None doubted that he was born with a good destiny. Accordingly he was named after his father, who had risen from the status of sharecropper to a nationally acclaimed minister and an esteemed leader in the black community of Atlanta, Georgia. Nurtured and protected by an intergenerational family all of his life, never having been in want of material resources even during the Great Depression, Martin Luther King Jr. was among the most privileged African Americans of his day. The symbiotic functions of his family, church, and school were continued when he entered prestigious Morehouse College, long committed to the training of African American male leaders imbued with a mission of service to the African American community. In that context, King's teachers and moral exemplars were some of African America's most talented academic scholars and "race leaders," not least of whom were Benjamin Mays, Howard Thurman, and George Kelsey, to mention only a few.

King's beneficence was also seen in a variety of personal traits, namely, his love of family, his deep loyalty to the well-being of his people, his belief in the equality of all peoples, and his embrace of the major traditions of his people as mediated to him through family, school, church, and college. Further, as a leader of his people in the struggle against racial oppression, which brought America's race problem and his movement to worldwide visibility, King's beneficent spirit was expressed in his unrelenting commitment to the philosophy of nonviolent resistance, his strong belief in the redemptive power of unmerited suffering, his untiring devotion to the principle of loving one's enemies, his consistent view that nobody is beyond the pale of moral transformation, and his steadfast faith that love and justice will ultimately prevail over evil.

Finally, King was the founder of the Southern Christian Leadership Conference, which institutionalized the principles that guided the thought and practice of the Civil Rights Movement he led. King and his organization soon became a source of moral power for peaceful social change in the United States. All who participated in the practices of nonviolent resistance were morally changed by them and gradually formed in accordance with the virtue of beneficence.

The converse of beneficence is, of course, the vice of meanness. Synonyms for meanness are small-mindedness, mean-spiritedness, disdain, contempt of others, self-centeredness, selfishness. The corresponding leadership style is that of the dictator, whose primary purpose is to make the needs of the community subservient to those of his or her own. Such a style is aloof, haughty, disdainful, arrogant, conceited, and wholly destructive of community, quintessential qualities of the philosophy of possessive individualism.[1]

Forbearance

Forbearance is an important moral virtue for Africans and African Americans because both have been bearers of a tragic destiny for many generations. That is, each has had to endure a long-term dehumanizing plight of racial oppression, economic injustice, political disfranchisement, and social ostracism. For generations their children were born into the cauldron of human degradation, cursed by conditions of suffering and deprivation. They did not (and often still do not) have access to the necessary resources with which to effect any radical change in their respective situations. Under such bitter conditions, moral development was closely allied with the struggle for survival, and moral character was gradually formed in accordance with the virtue of forbearance.

Because it helps people to survive dehumanizing conditions, forbearance can be one of the most effective means for preserving and promoting the goal of community. Patience and tolerance are two of its main synonyms. Yet the activities leading to its realization can be easily misunderstood as implying either complacency or contentment with one's situation. Rather, it may in fact be the case that, after careful deliberation about possible responses to a miserable situation, the simple act of *waiting* may be the best of all possible strategies. Doing what is necessary to preserve life under caustic conditions need not be viewed as either mindless submission or cowardice but, instead, as intelligent action. The collective wisdom of those who have lived for generations under such conditions may often be the most credible support for the spirit and practice of forbearance.

Activities that serve the pragmatic goal of survival are often the habits necessary for developing the virtue of forbearance. Under the most oppressive conditions, all forms of resistance are inevitably forced into concealment, as was commonplace during the periods of slavery and colonialism. Yet their subversive activities were often the principal means by which the people preserved their loyalty to the principal goal of their respective communities, the pursuit of freedom. Those who became outwardly rebellious, however, often lost their lives at an early age. Others who continuously resisted engagement with any such dissidence tended to develop character traits that in some respects were almost identical with those of their oppressors. That is to say, they eventually grew to hate their own people and, in different ways, they tended to blame their own race for all of their problems. Thus, to a great extent, they assumed the spirituality of their oppressors.[2]

During his many years in prison, Nelson Mandela chose to concentrate his activities on survival skills for himself, coupled with continuing his leadership from prison in the anti-apartheid struggle. He never lost sight of the goal in the service of which he had been sentenced to life in prison. Nevertheless, he became a person of forbearance by doing whatever he could in many concealed ways to aid his compatriots in the struggle. Since most of his fellow inmates at Robbin Island were political prisoners, it eventually came to be known as a training base for the underground activities of the ANC. I have heard several say that they rejoiced in being sentenced to Robbin Island because it was like going to a graduate school of education to study with the world's most esteemed scholar. There for the first time they would meet and learn directly from Mandela, a man whose name, picture, and words were banned throughout South Africa. Interestingly, all such efforts to obliterate the man's leadership only added to his mystique and in turn helped to unify all elements in the resistance movement.

Often leaders of freedom movements do not make good politicians because they are not easily disposed toward compromise. Mandela was different. On the one hand, he would never compromise on the principle of universal franchise for his people nor grant the government the right to the high moral ground by demanding that the ANC forsake its commitment to armed struggle. With respect to the latter, he said the following soon after his release from prison:

> The renunciation of violence by either the government or the ANC should not be a precondition to but the result of

negotiation. . . . The position of the ANC on the question of violence is, therefore, very clear. A government which used violence against blacks many years before we took up arms has no right whatsoever to call on us to lay down arms.[3]

On the other hand, Mandela was willing to compromise with then-President F. W. deKlerk in ways so politically astute that the world was amazed. I claim that his capacity to hold on to certain essential principles while compromising on other matters exhibits the virtue of forbearance, which held him in good stead during his imprisonment and which prepared him well for his later role in negotiating the demise of apartheid.

Similarly, Martin Luther King Jr. possessed the virtue of forbearance. The initial way in which he and his associates responded to the arrest of Rosa Parks reveals the content of the virtue. At first, the Montgomery Improvement Association, headed by King, did not challenge the system of racial segregation as such but merely requested modest improvement in the management of segregated buses. King and most of his followers, having endured racial segregation and discrimination all their lives, had been trained from childhood onward in customary habits of dealing with it. Most felt it was an unchangeable social structure strongly supported by the terrorizing activities of the Ku Klux Klan and bent on coercing compliance with the system through mass fear and intimidation. In my judgment the virtue of forbearance resulted from long-standing practices among African Americans, extending back to the earliest days of slavery on the continent of Africa.

Undoubtedly, one tradition that this virtue inspired was the so-called accommodationist leadership style of Booker T. Washington, whose influential leadership was a dominant force in the public life of African Americans throughout the first two decades of the twentieth century. That legacy, which Washington himself inherited from his teachers and mentors, has lived on in succeeding generations as symbolized in the many schools throughout the south that continue to bear his name.

The virtue of forbearance also enabled both Africans and African Americans to give their assent to the philosophy of nonviolent resistance long before it was named and articulated as such by Mahatma Gandhi. That is to say, it was not the philosophy of nonviolent resistance that inspired people's acceptance of it. Rather, it was generations of nonviolent practices that culminated in the virtue of forbearance and motivated people's acceptance of nonviolence resistance as a philosophy. The novelty of its use by King was that of direct public confrontation with the white power structure rather than the older activities of indirect subversion.

In sum, the leadership of both Nelson Mandela and Martin Luther King Jr. involved their courageous commitment on the one hand to uncompromising legal principles vis-à-vis the issues of disfranchisement, racial segregation, and discrimination and on the other hand to varying forms of pragmatic compromises vis-à-vis public policy strategies.

The converse of the virtue of forbearance is that of impatience or intolerance, which leads to either foolish and impulsive activities or acquiescence. The former is likely to contribute to a retaliatory style of leadership, while the latter invariably produces reactionary leadership.

Practical Wisdom

Practical wisdom is excellence of thought that guides good action. This virtue pertains to the measure of cognitive discernment necessary for determining what hinders good action and what enables it. It is the fully developed capacity of a free moral agent for making reasonable judgments about the best means for the attainment of penultimate goals as well as the determination of their commensurability with the ultimate goal of the good life. As with all the virtues practical wisdom is acquired by example and practice. For instance, proper training requires exposing children to the influence of persons of practical wisdom. That is, children need to be in the care of such people for a long time to observe them as models and emulate their activities. Children imitate the activities and styles of their primary mentors—parents, older siblings, adult family members, teachers.

Africans and African Americans highly value the wisdom of their elders because of its grounding in a reservoir of experience. Africans are convinced that the normative value of tradition is embodied in those who have lived to see old age and are now close to the transition to the ancestral world. In their upbringing, most African parents assume that their children will be significantly related to the generation of their grandparents and possibly even that of their great-grandparents. Unfortunately, the conditions of modern urban life have often militated against the full realization of this reality. Similarly, African Americans have assumed the important presence of intergenerational adults in the upbringing of their children. Whenever their children were separated from their grandparents by geography (as when African Americans had emigrated to the cities), many generations of parents sent their children to live with their grandparents during school holidays.

Since time is needed for the efficacy of personal influence, spending the summer in the care of grandparents enabled children to learn about their values and to experience the practical import of those values.

Practical wisdom pertains to intelligent discernment. Most important, the person of practical wisdom is able to relate the values of the tradition appropriately to particular situations. A good example of this power is the ability to bring proverbial knowledge to bear on particular contexts as a cultural tool of education and enlightenment. Sometimes that ability is acquired even by the young and especially when they are exposed to proverbial teaching, as Sylvanus Udoidem relates:

> Among the Ibibio, if a young person uses many *Nke* [proverbs] to flavour his discussion or drive home his argument, he is often looked upon as "*Eyen Akan-eren*" ("the son of an old man"). This is not meant in a literal or biological sense. . . . What the expression means is that such a speaker has taken possession of the linguistic inheritance

bequeathed to his generation by the older ones. Such individuals are considered . . . knowledgeable, wise, sophisticated, versatile and having a moral character on whom the elders can rely for the continuity of the shared values of the people.[4]

Like all the virtues, practical wisdom is the excellent exercise of a skill. Since it pertains to the art of discerning the best means to the attainment of goals, it is calculative in nature. The person of practical wisdom must weigh options and choose the best of them. In the process the person must also calculate the extent to which the substance of the deliberations should be made public or concealed. Poor judgment with respect to either may damage the outcome's acceptability. A person of practical wisdom also knows when to end the deliberative process and make a decision. Discerning the right time to act is an important part of the process.

Practical wisdom is essential for the whole of moral virtue and for all good leadership because it provides the reasoning underlying all the virtues. Practical wisdom enables excellence in judgment. The person of practical wisdom must be knowledgeable about the cultural tradition, as a scholar might be. More important, that person must know how to relate the traditional wisdom of the ages to the particular issues at hand and to do so in such a way that reasonable persons throughout the community will see and approve the integrity of the judgment. Thus, before passing judgment, the person of practical wisdom must listen carefully to all who have relevant information pertaining to the issue at hand. Such a person must be open-minded. He or she must shun premature closure. Since the problems at hand are likely to be divisive within the community, the person of practical wisdom seeks a solution that reconstitutes the unity of the community without any undue sacrifice.

Undoubtedly, all would agree that both Nelson Mandela and Martin Luther King Jr. were men of practical wisdom. From childhood, both "drank deeply," so to speak, from their respective cultural traditions. Both were nurtured in intergenerational families, and in those contexts they were exposed in various ways to the best leaders and mentors of their day. Both had the opportunity to exercise leadership in the youth divisions of the communal organizations in which their elders were visibly active.[5] At an early age both gained experience as peer leaders and impressed all who observed them as intelligent, trustworthy young men with great potential for moral leadership. Mandela's practical wisdom was most manifest in his negotiating skills with his former enemies, King's in his crafting and delivery of persuasive public speeches.

The converse of practical wisdom is simply natural instinct, which issues in impulsive activities that are both unreasonable and uncontrolled. Such people are easily provoked to anger, and their leadership style is necessarily erratic.

Improvisation

Moral virtues are like the arts. They are formed by habitual practice. Although they adhere to certain common patterns, mere imitation alone can produce neither morally virtuous persons nor great artists. Rather, the practices that produce either the virtue or the art must become like a second nature made distinctive by the individuality of the person. Thus the person becomes formed by the practice and exhibits that form in a novel way. The novelty represents the actor's unique mark.

Although African and African American families have high regard for tradition, they are also lovers of creative ventures and especially those that expand upon a prescribed theme. Such is the nature of improvisation, which reaches its zenith in musical, oratorical, and ceremonial performance. Among African peoples, one sees signs of improvisation almost everywhere, from the mundane affairs of life to the sublime. In all parts of Africa one is constantly amazed by the high degree of human ingenuity displayed in the day-to-day activities of ordinary life. The way in which music, dancing, and singing are integrated into the activity of work contributes energy and beauty to the improvisational and cooperative spirit of the

people involved. Westerners visiting anywhere in Africa can be constantly sur-
prised in observing the improvisational
work of African auto mechanics repairing
engine difficulties with limited tools and
few if any spare parts. Such skills are truly
inventive. Since poverty constitutes a
basic condition for many improvisational
practices, African peoples bestow much
praise on the authors of invention, because, more often than not, their product
represents the creation of something new
out of virtually nothing.

One of the most significant spheres of
creativity in Africa is that of proverbs. The
ability to speak in proverbs is a creative
art, as is the ability to understand it.
Proverbs are examples *par excellence* of
improvised activities. They tend both to
affirm and to violate customary rules.
Udoidem's analysis of proverbs shows
how their origin and function are analogous to the activities that culminate in the
virtue of improvisation:

> Proverbs promote the recovery of order
> through a new context. The creativity
> that is involved goes beyond proposing

new meanings—it reorganizes our vision of reality. A proverb serves as an occasion for creative reflection: it is a framework for collaborative and contributive creativity both for the speaker and the listener. The former gains a new insight into the given situation that necessitates the application of a particular proverb. For the latter, this provides a frame for reflection, creative insight and an awareness of a new reality. A proverb helps the mind to become investigative and creative. . . . Proverbalization is thus a private and relatively unstructured process that results in the creation of new ideas and insights.[6]

Improvisation comprises unpredictable variations on a theme. It brings novelty to bear on the familiar not for the sake of destroying the latter but for the purpose of heightening the individuality and uniqueness of the agent and his or her creative ability. Improvisation expresses not only the agent's creativity and spontaneity but also his or her spirit of perceptive wholeness. By keeping the old and new close at hand, the virtue of improvisation embraces and enhances the whole and thus serves to promote and preserve the goal of community.

The art of improvisation appears throughout the cultural history of African Americans to such an extent that some have claimed that a powerful aesthetic quality inheres in the race itself. If aesthetics is understood as the attempt to make life better, then the traditions of African peoples have always aimed at that goal. Dealing constantly with the tragic elements of life, Africans have traditionally sought to make life more pleasant through the cultivation of the visual and auditory arts. Drawings, paintings, sculptures are everywhere abundant, from the most remote village to the densest urban centers. Similarly, music and dance in their intense creative polyrhythmic forms are designed to help the people in every possible circumstance of life. African arts are to enhance the everyday life of the people, not primarily to change their conditions but to enable the people to see and hear and feel beauty. As long as the people enjoy beauty, they do not succumb to the tragic elements in their midst. Their spirits are uplifted, and in that way the arts preserve and promote the well-being of the community.

All creative activities are commensurate with this art of improvisation. Moral formation and political leadership are not exceptions. Nelson Mandela's embodiment of the virtue of improvisation was seen in his consistent activities aimed at remolding both the old system of racial oppression and its perpetrators into a newly expansive "nonracial" community. The vision of the latter includes the former oppressors united in a thoroughly reorganized and reconstituted system. The virtue of improvisation was acquired by Mandela from the teachings and examples of his predecessors and contemporaries alike (several of whom he did not hesitate to name time and time again, such as Robert Subukwe, John Dube, Josiah Gumede, G. M. Naicker, Chief Luthuli, Chris Hani, and Oliver Tambo). Clearly, too, Mandela's activities inspired the improvisational activities of countless others in drama, music, dance, song, as well as numerous types of community organizational work throughout the nation.

Martin Luther King Jr.'s embodiment of the virtue of improvisation is seen primarily in the excellence of his oratorical skills, whereby he was able to infuse new meanings into old traditions and remake them into suitable bearers of a new public morality. Like Mandela, King acquired the virtue of improvisation from his teachers and mentors. Similarly, a whole generation of people was inspired to improvisational activities by extending the principles of his work to many other causes. His work also provided the inspiration for creative advances in the arts and in all levels of political involvement.

The converse of the virtue of improvisation is rigidity, fixity, legalism, dogmatism, all of which connote an incapacity for creativity and an insensitivity to the psychic needs of oppressed peoples. All such leaders can only imitate prescribed patterns. Their leadership is invariably robotic, and their capabilities are limited to the performance of only routinized functions.

Forgiveness

After centuries of racial oppression one can rightly ask why African peoples seem to exhibit such little racial hatred in return for the misery they were forced to endure. Even during the most intense periods of resistance to slavery, segregation, colonialism, and apartheid, they have rarely been consumed by the spirit of hatred. How did they escape such a destiny? This is an important question, worthy of the most careful investigation, although beyond the scope of this study. Suffice it to say that the commitment of African peoples to the goal of community is one of the principal reasons for the lack of racial hatred among them. The goal of their life is to build relationships rather than prohibit them; this has had an enormous effect on their moral formation.

African peoples have always known the great toll that hatred takes on both the personality of individuals and the life of the community. In the interest of their highest goal, community, they have shunned hatred by cultivating the virtue of forgiveness through the habitual exercise of kindness.

Even in defeat, however, Africans have always admired the technological superiority of European peoples, which, like their own powers, they believed to be deeply rooted in the realm of invisible spirit. Thus they knew that all warfare between themselves and Europeans would necessarily be cosmological in nature. Since most of their traditional attempts to expunge the western invader by force had failed, they felt obliged to forbear and wait for the proper time when it would be possible to rid themselves of European domination by means other than warfare. In the meantime they would do whatever was possible to cultivate the seed of resistance in many and varied concealed ways. By the middle of the twentieth century the right time had arrived, and their goal of political independence was close at hand. At the same time a similar circumstance was appearing in the historical struggle of African Americans for racial justice.

The virtue of forgiveness is essential for the ongoing life of community. For countless reasons, humans inevitably fail to do the good that they are capable of doing. The results of those failures can and often do threaten the well-being of others. Traditionally Africans faced such circumstances by seeking effective means for the restoration of the spiritual balance upset by the pernicious activity. Only then could reconciliation occur between the parties involved. As we have seen, since all activities in Africa are integrally related to all the realms of life, the reconciliation had to be similarly inclusive of all the grieved parties.

The breaking of taboos constituted the most severe threat to the community's well-being. In such cases, restoration of the balance required a major sacrifice, usually the life of the wrongdoer. Such an act was not viewed as merely retaliatory but as a necessary and effective means for reconciliation with all the offended persons, spirits, and divinities.

Thus traditional African societies knew much about forgiveness and what it entailed for both individuals and the community alike. Consequently, Africans did not harbor long-term resentments against anybody. They instead sought to resolve the problems as quickly as possible so as not to be exposed to the spiritual imbalance for too long a time. In their relations with slaveholders and colonialists, African peoples entered into various types of communal relationships with them all along the way. As servants they attended to all their oppressors' personal needs, often living with them under the same roof or in the same compound. Through involuntary sexual liaisons African women on the continent and in the diaspora have given birth to a mixed race of people. Eventually small numbers of the conquered ones were formally educated in the foreigner's cultural traditions. These and numerous other practices knitted the two groups together in an ambiguous way. Yet no such unity, ambiguous as it was, could have been possible without the forgiveness of the African peoples for their long night of sorrow and misery. From then until now, Africans have striven for the expansion of community in which the two races might be able to live together in mutual respect.

It may be that many of the continuing problems between the two rest on the fact that the Europeans never asked the Africans for their forgiveness. That is to say, they never repented of their evil deeds or attempted to compensate their victims for their losses.

Nelson Mandela's approach to the virtue of forgiveness is instructive. Despite serving twenty-seven years in prison for his pursuit of a just cause, he exhibited no detectable signs of racial hatred. Rather, the spirit of dignity and good will that he revealed to the world on the day of his release from prison was the same spirit that African peoples have been extending to their oppressors for many generations. It did not surprise Africans anywhere that he had the capacity to forgive his oppressors and to negotiate with them in good faith. He laid down only one condition, however: that those with whom he negotiated would be persons of integrity. He believed that then-President deKlerk was such a person. It was a belief about which he had some second thoughts at one point in the process, when the negotiations were seriously threatened by reports of the complicity of the South African police force in fomenting violence. Mandela's confidence in deKlerk was soon restored by the latter's reactions to those charges. Clearly some measure of repentance is a precondition for the efficacy of forgiveness.

Similarly, Martin Luther King Jr. was imbued with the virtue of forgiveness. When his home was bombed for the first time (with his wife and baby daughter in a room next to the blast), he calmed the angry crowd that gathered, imploring them to fight violence not with violence but with the spirit of nonviolence, which functioned for him as a philosophy of forgiveness. Time and again he reiterated his teaching that African Americans were called to hate the evil but not the evildoer, that they should never give up the idea that evildoers are capable of moral transformation.

The virtue of forgiveness was reflected in the leadership style of both men. It is no accident that Mandela's new government took as its motto *reconciliation and unity,* invoking two key political principles that signaled the ultimate goal of the new South Africa. These political principles gained credibility in large part because of their embodiment in the character of Mandela himself.

The virtue of forgiveness was reflected in the leadership style of Martin Luther King Jr., who seemed to foretell that he would be assassinated some day. Yet his many speeches, including his final sermon the night before his death, were replete with the spirit of forgiveness, admonishing his followers to fight hate not with hate but with love and forgiveness. The way of love and forgiveness is not, as often thought, the way of weakness but the way of strength, because it is not a natural response but rather a response that manifests a second nature.

The converse of the virtue of forgiveness is the vice of hatred, which repudiates any possibility of reconciliation with one's enemies and which views one's enemies as demonic. The leadership style that emanates from such a vice is isolationist, chauvinist, and belligerent, easily disposed to acts of retaliation.

Contrary to such acts, which accept evil on its own terms, the virtue of forgiveness facilitates rising to a higher moral ground. For forgiveness to be workable, however, the instruments of violence must be tightly controlled through adequate structures of justice. King's practice of nonviolent resistance was practical because he could rely on such structures through the actions of the Supreme Court and the National Guard. But the African National Congress, fully committed to nonviolent resistance for fifty years, finally concluded that it was no longer workable because of the lack of such structures of justice for restraining violence. Thus, after the Sharpville Massacre in 1960, the ANC reluctantly decided that it was forced by the structures of violence to engage in armed struggle. In reflecting on that period, Mandela writes:

> The government knows only too well that there is not a single political organization in this country, inside or outside Parliament, which can ever compare with the ANC in its total commitment to peaceful change.

Right from the early days of its history, the organization diligently sought peaceful solutions and, to that extent, it talked patiently to successive South African governments, a policy we tried to follow in dealing with the present government.

Not only did the government ignore our demands for a meeting; instead it took advantage of our commitment to a nonviolent struggle and unleashed the most violent form of racial oppression this country has ever seen. It stripped us of all basic human rights, outlawed our organizations, and barred all channels of peaceful resistance. It met our demands with force and, despite the grave problems facing the country, it continues to refuse to talk to us. There can only be one answer to this challenge: violent forms of struggle.

Down through the years oppressed people have fought for their birthright by peaceful means, where that was possible, and through force, where peaceful channels were closed.[7]

Mandela's words clearly demonstrate the necessary conditions for the workability of nonviolent resistance. Neither Mahatma Gandhi nor Martin Luther King Jr. faced such ruthless disregard for human life as did Mandela and his African National Congress. Neither Gandhi nor King and their respective movements were banned from civil society.

Justice

A word must now be said about justice and whether it is for Africans and African Americans one of the moral virtues. I claim that it is the supreme virtue because it is the sum of all the virtues. On the one hand, it inheres in each of them by determining the moral impact of their practices on others. On the other hand, it is the totality of the moral quality contained in all the virtues. In other words, one cannot be just without possessing all the other virtues, because complete justice would be diminished by the lack of any one of them. Thus the virtues of beneficence, forbearance, practical wisdom, improvisation, and forgiveness and those that are not treated here are all practical activities, the exercise of which contributes not only to one's own good but, more important, to the good of the community. The latter is the ultimate goal of justice. In all human activities, African peoples are concerned primarily with two forms of justice: (1) the individual's obligations to the community as mediated through the many dealings individuals have with one another and (2) the community's obligations to its members and itself. Aristotle classified these two concerns as commutative and distributive justice, respectively, the former pertaining to civil law and the latter to the common good.

It is beyond the task of this study to present a full-scale African and African American understanding of justice. Suffice it to say, however, that the ultimate goal of justice is also the preservation and promotion of community. A distinctive feature of the African view of distributive justice is the substantive role that the community is expected to assume for the well-being of its members. Many have referred to this concern in traditional African society as African socialism or, more precisely, African communalism. Both terms connote a high degree of com-

munal ownership of basic material resources required by all citizens for a viable
life.

Because of the high moral value Africans
place on community as the ultimate goal
of all their activities and because of its integral relatedness to the various realms of
life, most Africans are favorably disposed
to the basic principles of socialist governments, while reluctant to transfer any particular political structure from a foreign
cultural context to their own. Their orien-
tation to socialist principles, then, owes
nothing to the philosophy of Karl Marx or
the ideology of communism as practiced
by the former Soviet Union or by other
modern governments. Rather, its grounding lies in the cosmological thought of
traditional African societies. Such thought
is fundamentally different from that of
western Enlightenment political philosophies, which are primarily interested in
protecting individual rights and private
property. The latter philosophies necessarily presuppose contractual societies that,
unlike communal societies, cannot take
for granted the protection of individuals.
Theories of human rights are necessarily

constructed, and their legalization becomes foundational for all such contractual societies. An inevitable problem emerges, however, whenever the latter seeks to impose its moral system of thought onto countries not constituted according to theories of political contract.

As with all the virtues, African understandings of justice are regulated by the demands of their ultimate goal, namely, the preservation and promotion of community. Such a goal requires a basic structure of inclusive equality, wherein the well-being of all the community's members is assured. This does not imply any form of absolute egalitarianism since the hierarchical ordering of African societies insists on many levels of inequality based on moral and political distinctions with respect to the differing contributions each makes to the well-being of the whole community.

In terms of his leadership, Mandela's program of Reconstruction and Development reflected his commitment to a communal understanding of justice. His government did not draw sharp lines of demarcation between, on the one hand, formal laws of rights and opportunities and, on the other, public policies of material assistance and entitlements.

At the time of his death, King was preparing to lead a march on Washington protesting the plight of the nation's poor and calling upon the government to assume responsibility for the elimination of poverty. His organization of the nation's diverse poor into the Poor People's Campaign and his numerous speeches, informal conversations, and close personal associations have provided evidence for some scholars to claim that he was a so-called closeted socialist.[8] In my judgment, King's political philosophy was based on his strong belief in the "beloved community" as the final goal of all human endeavor. In his philosophy, government has an obligation to provide for the legal protection as well as the material necessities of its citizenry.

Public and Private Ethics

The foregoing analysis of six African and African American virtues, namely, beneficence, forbearance, practical wisdom, improvisation, forgiveness, and justice, has demonstrated their deep roots in the cultural traditions of African peoples. Although not comprehensive, I hope that discussion of six of them is adequate to illustrate the theory of African and African American ethics.

Demonstrating the personal and public character of African and African American ethics has been a necessary methodological requirement because the ethic I have sought to explicate is primarily a public one. Its *telos* or goal is inherently public, namely, the preservation and promotion of community. By illustrating the embodiment of all six virtues in two major international figures, President Nelson Rolihlahla Mandela and Dr. Martin Luther King Jr., I have made a plausible argument in support of my claim that these two persons, one African and the other African American, shared a common worldview and embodied a common morality. Further, they have both greatly inspired countless millions around the world to embrace their respective visions of social justice as well as their moral endeavors for its realization. Further still, I have endeavored to show how each of the virtues they embodied expressed itself in their public practices. By doing so, I hope I have signaled the implications of this ethic for public policy and especially how each was able either to reappropriate or to reconstitute the Eurocentric traditions of their respective societies.

Yet I cannot overemphasize the fact that my intent in drawing upon Mr. Mandela and Dr. King is to illustrate an African and African American ethic that is in no way limited to these two leaders. I hope that none will misunderstand this aim.

All of the virtues that I have discussed are royal virtues. That is, they are the virtues befitting the character of most traditional African kings and queens, who have been wrongly understood as despots. They were, rather, mediators between the tribal community and the world of spirit. Their traditional role was always to strive to maintain all the proper relationships among the many and varied forces on which the community's well-being depended. Further and most important, these

royal virtues have always been widely dis-
tributed within African communities, lay-
ing claims on each member to aspire to
their realization in his or her moral development. Every member of the community
was expected to develop the moral nature
of a good king or a good queen. A community of such moral integrity guaranteed
its preservation. Thus the ethic has pragmatic value.

Finally, given the negative disposition
Americans have had toward royalty, at
least since the American Revolution, it is
important to say a word in defense of the
term *royal*. African traditions cannot be
understood or appreciated apart from a
clear grasp of this reality. Admittedly,
there are good kings and bad kings, good
queens and bad queens. Although not all
traditional African societies had monar-
chies, alternative structures provided similar forms of authority. Sometimes the
paramount authority was located in a
council of chiefs. Under such circumstances, the function of the council was
not unlike that of the traditional king. In
any case, societies were hierarchically

ordered, with numerous checks and balances against despotism, which was always considered the worst form of evil that could possibly befall a people. Whenever despots emerged, however, traditional societies had effective ways for the removal of such persons from office, usually by ceremonial sacrifice. Many military coups in modern-day Africa should be understood in this light. When political corruption becomes so extensive as to stifle the strivings of the masses for a viable life, the latter have often rejoiced and praised the military for bringing them relief from their suffering. But when the military merely replaces the despotism of the former by its own arbitrary governance, then the condition of the people can worsen.

American scholars have long been puzzled in their attempts to explain the immense authority exercised by the typical African American pastor. Since the vast majority of African American churches have a congregational type of polity, it is all the more puzzling to explain why the pastor has as much authority as he or she does. Unfortunately, the widespread use (by sociologists and others) of Max Weber's category of charismatic leadership to explain this phenomenon has become almost commonplace. In my judgment, such a concept fails to do justice to the phenomenon. A far more adequate explanation for the pastor's status lies in an understanding of African kingship and the way its moral substance has been transmitted to America through the role and function of African American religious leaders. Their congregations assume the space of a tribal community, and they themselves imbue the tribal chief or king with a wide breadth of authoritative powers.

4

The Christian Factor in African and African American Social Ethics

Christianity and Islam are two guest religions on the African continent that are continuing to undergo the process of syncretism with traditional African cultural thought and practice.[1] That process has been called many names, the most frequent being "Africanization," "enculturation," "indigenization," and "decolonization." Regardless of the name, however, the goal is the same, namely that of enculturating Christianity so that Africans will cease viewing it as a lingering legacy of the cultural imperialism of European colonialism. Unlike Islam, however, and though undertaken unwittingly, Christians' practice of translating Christianity into African languages has greatly facilitated that process.[2]

Traditionally, Africans on the continent and in the diaspora have searched the biblical scriptures for positive references to African peoples.[3] From the earliest times they have taken great comfort in the text that has been a keystone for all African Christian nationalism, namely, Psalm 68:31, "Princes shall come out of Egypt; Ethiopia shall soon stretch out her hands unto God." In varying ways this text became the justifying source for the so-called Ethiopian Movement that swept the African continent from the 1880s onward. A century earlier it had been a source of inspiration for the African American Independent Church Movement. The principal aims of both movements were two: (1) resistance to racism, slavery, and colonialism, and (2) advocacy for the independence of African churches from European control. Unfortunately, both movements were greeted by their opponents with extreme measures of political, legal, and military repression. The British, for example, imprisoned and executed several Christian prophets of this movement, including Prophet John Chilembwe of Malawi, who was executed in 1915, and Prophet Simon Kimbangu (founder of the Church of Jesus Christ of the Prophet Simon Kimbangu), who was imprisoned in the former Belgian Congo from 1921 until his death in 1951.[4] Most independence movements in African and nationalist movements in the diaspora have claimed some measure of inspiration from Psalm 68:31.

The African American Independent Church movement emerged with the founding of the African Methodist Episcopal Church, the African Methodist Episcopal Zion Church, and the African Episcopal Church in the 1790s. In 1805 Thomas Paul organized the African Baptist Church in Boston, and, along with a group of Ethiopian traders who had resisted the segregated seating patterns of the white Baptist church in New York, he organized the Abyssinian Baptist Church in New York City in 1808. The following year, the First African Baptist Church in Philadelphia was founded. The spirit of this African American independence movement as affirmed by the vast majority of

African Americans was commensurate with that of the Ethiopian Movement almost a century later.

The founding of the Liberian settlement of repatriated American slaves in 1820, as well as the colonization of Sierra Leone by returned slaves from Nova Scotia in 1792, contained similar nationalist elements that reflected the spirituality of their peoples in the common quest for an independent space in which to pursue their goal of community-building.

Ethiopia's almost unique status, having been one of only two African countries never to have fallen under the yoke of European colonial rule, added immense significance to her near-sacred status among African peoples everywhere. Further, the import of Ethiopianism was enhanced by the symbol of its throne and the resplendent majesty of its emperor, who traced his descent back through Queen Cleopatra to the Queen of Sheba, the wife of King Solomon. Additionally, the emperor's titles included that of Defender of the Faith and Head of the Ethiopian Orthodox Church, which tradition claimed had been founded by St. Thomas the Apostle.

No visit by any head of government has ever captured the imagination and pride of African Americans like that of His Imperial Majesty Haile Selassie's visit to New York City in the 1930s. His gift to the Abyssinian Baptist Church of a six-foot silver cross is firmly embedded in the pulpit area of the present edifice. In Trinidad, Jamaica, and other parts of the Caribbean, the Rastafarian Movement[5] once claimed the Emperor Haile Selassie as the Living God of his followers, the Ras Tafari. The Movement believes that salvation comes only to those who are repatriated to Africa and live under the sovereign rule of African governments. The Rastafarians also claim continuity in philosophy and theology with Marcus Garvey's Back to Africa Movement, the largest African American social movement ever to arise in the United States. During its rapid ascent to national visibility in the 1920s, it spread throughout the United States, Canada, and the Caribbean with the blessing of George Alexander McGuire, first Patriarch of the African Orthodox Church, a branch of which still survives in my native town of Sydney in the province of

Nova Scotia. All contemporary black nationalist and Pan-African movements exhibit many similarities with the Garvey Movement.

Inspired by the independence of Ghana in 1957 under the charismatic leadership of Kwame Nkrumah, black consciousness movements in the United States emerged and soon spread to Canada and linked up with similar movements in South Africa in the late 1960s and early 70s. All exhibited the common goals of freedom and empowerment for African peoples. The spirit of these movements has permeated African cultures everywhere, redeeming them from centuries of conquest by the restoration of political independence and the recovery of personal dignity. The many and varied corresponding activities of African peoples on the continent and in the diaspora have been both complementary and encouraging resources for one another.

Greatly enabled by the rapid technological developments in communications, African peoples are in closer contact with one another than was ever thought possible even a quarter of a century ago. Only in the twentieth century have Africans come to the Americas voluntarily, and in the last half of the twentieth century they have been coming in ever-increasing numbers. Similarly, in recent decades, large numbers of African Americans have been traveling back and forth to Africa in large numbers. The full cultural impact of such face-to-face encounters is hard to estimate. Suffice it to say that the cultural impact is already being felt in music, dance, religion, and the visual arts. Clearly African peoples are rapidly discovering the enormous cultural resources they may yet contribute to the enrichment of one another's lives.

Most Africans on the continent now claim Christianity as their own. Even though the gradual process of enculturation continues unabated in the independent African churches,[6] it is often greatly hindered by the various controlling forces that many former mission churches continue to exert on their denominational counterparts in Africa. Yet the handwriting is on the wall, so to speak, and sooner or later, like African American Christianity, African Christianity will also emerge full-blown as a distinctive contribution to the newly emerging world Christianity.

Notes

1. The African Factor in the African American Experience

1. For a full discussion of this ritual, see J. Osmosade Awolalu, *Yoruba Beliefs and Sacrificial Rites* (London: Longman, 1979), 152–56.

2. Henry Louis Gates Jr., *The Signifying Monkey: A Theory of African-American Literary Criticism* (New York: Oxford University Press, 1988), 63–64.

2. Virtue Theory

1. This insight is supported by the work of Robert M. Franklin. His book *Liberating Visions: Human Fulfillment and Social Justice in African-American Thought* (Minneapolis: Fortress Press, 1990) constitutes an important ethical inquiry into the lives of four major African American leaders in order to explicate the integral relatedness of the personal and public dimensions of their respective thought and action.

2. If *original sin* refers to violation of things that are forbidden by God, then the African understanding of taboo may be its closest equivalent. E. Bolaji Idowu names adultery, beating one's parent, and breaking a covenant as taboo. See his

Ododumare: God in Yoruba Belief (London: Longman, 1962), 144ff.

3. In my judgment most African American ethicists have discerned the importance of culture for African American ethics. Hence many of their works have assumed the form of cultural analyses in search of the basic elements of an African American social ethic. This judgment applies to the following: Garth Baker-Fletcher, *Somebodyness: Martin Luther King, Jr., and the Theory of Dignity* (Minneapolis: Fortress Press, 1993); Lewis V. Baldwin, *There Is a Balm in Gilead: The Cultural Roots of Martin Luther King, Jr.* (Minneapolis: Fortress Press, 1991) and *To Make the Wounded Whole: The Cultural Legacy of Martin Luther King, Jr.* (Minneapolis: Fortress Press, 1992); Katie G. Cannon, *Black Womanist Ethics* (Atlanta: Scholars, 1988); Riggins R. Earl Jr., *Dark Symbols, Obscure Signs: God, Self, and Community in the Slave Mind* (Maryknoll, N.Y.: Orbis, 1993); Franklin, *Liberating Visions*; Enoch H. Oglesby, *Ethics and Theology from the Other Side: Sounds of Moral Struggle* (Washington, D.C.: University Press of America, 1990) and *Born in the Fire: Case Studies in Christian Ethics and Globalization* (New York: Pilgrim, 1990); Peter J. Paris, *The Social Teaching of the Black Churches* (Philadelphia: Fortress Press, 1985) and *Black Religious Leaders: Conflict in Unity* (Louisville, Ky.: Westminster John Knox, 1992); Archie Smith Jr., *The Relational Self: Ethics and Theory from a Black Church Perspective* (Nashville: Abingdon, 1982); Erwin Smith, *The Ethics of Martin Luther King, Jr.* (Toronto: Edwin Mellen, 1981); Emilie M. Townes, *Womanist Justice, Womanist Hope* (Atlanta: Scholars, 1993). See also Marcia Y.

Riggs, "'A Clarion Call to Awake! Arise! Act!' The Response of the Black Women's Club Movement to Institutionalized Moral Evil," and M. Shawn Copeland, "'Wading through Many Sorrows': Toward a Theology of Suffering in Womanist Perspective," in Emilie M. Townes, ed., *A Troubling in My Soul: Womanist Perspectives on Evil and Suffering* (Maryknoll, N.Y.: Orbis, 1993); Theodore Walker Jr., *Empower the People: Social Ethics for the African-American Church* (Maryknoll, N.Y.: Orbis, 1991); Gayraud S. Wilmore, *Black Religion and Black Radicalism: An Interpretation of the Religious History of the Afro-American People,* 3rd ed. (Maryknoll, N.Y.: Orbis, 2000); Preston N. Williams, "Contextualizing the Faith: The African-American Tradition and Martin Luther King, Jr.," in Ruy Costa, ed., *One Faith, Many Cultures* (Maryknoll, N.Y.: Orbis, 1988).

4. This does not preclude certain similarities between African and African American virtues and those of other traditions. Readers will detect some correspondence with Aristotle's ethics and especially the relation of the latter to the major science of his *Politics.* But readers will quickly discern major methodological differences between our ethic and that of Stanley Hauerwas, whose Christian ethics assumes no direct responsibility for political engagement. See especially his books *Character and the Christian Life: A Study in Theological Ethics* (San Antonio: Trinity University Press, 1985) and *The Peaceable Kingdom: A Primer in Christian Ethics* (Notre Dame, Ind.: University of Notre Dame Press, 1984). I am convinced that his pessimism about the incommensurability of virtue ethics in a pluralistic society is contradicted by the

transformative actions of leaders like President Nelson Mandela and Dr. Martin Luther King Jr., both of whom have been exemplars of virtue ethics as well as effective negotiators for social change in their respective pluralistic societies.

5. All virtue ethics require a primary moral goal that is reflected in a set of canonical virtues. Virtues are types of moral excellence. All citizens and especially all public officers are expected to possess that set of moral virtues, which are further bolstered and encouraged by official respect and praise. They are acquired by proper training and habitual practice.

The western tradition of virtue ethics is derived from Plato and Aristotle. Plato's virtues, later called the cardinal virtues by Christian tradition, are four—namely, temperance, courage, prudence, and justice. Plato's virtues are ideal forms. Building on the ideal Platonic virtues, Augustine claimed that God was the source of the virtues and their final end. Augustine viewed the moral life as faith in Jesus Christ and obedience to the dictates of God. By identifying God with the true end of human action, ethics becomes deductive inquiry that begins with the being of God rather than the strivings of humans. From this line of Platonic thinking the Christian virtues were understood as supernatural and transcendent of human strivings.

Aristotle's ethics was quite different; his method was inductive rather than deductive. In his view ethics involved a scientific inquiry into the ethos of particular communities. Thus ethics was culturally specific, dealing with the kind of virtues that the culture nurtured and encouraged. Further, in Aristotle's approach ethics and politics are part of the same inquiry because the final goal of individuals and that of the state are the same. Further, the person of complete virtue was capable of ruling the others because that person not only was morally good but also knew how to effect the good for others.

Thomas Aquinas's method was that of synthesizing the Aristotelian view of the virtues with that of Augustinian tradition by identifying the three Christian virtues of faith, hope, and love as supernatural virtues that complemented the natural cardinal virtues.

Many modern virtue ethicists have much in common with the Platonic and Augustinian tradition. My approach, however, differs from theirs in being more closely related to the Aristotelian tradition, in view of the cultural specificity of African and African American ethics. This does not necessarily imply parochialism. Rather it is my claim that the breadth and depth of community can only be determined politically. The capacity of communities to be open to expansion is also determined by their cultural traditions. Finally, readers will find in this study no attempt to impose any Aristotelian framework of thought onto our subject matter. I have instead discovered a small number of methodological similarities between the ethics of Africans and African Americans and that of Aristotle. Yet the two remain very different in many ways.

6. Again, readers of Aristotle's *Nicomachean Ethics* and *Politics* will easily recognize his shadow in many parts of this text. Since Aristotle's theory of moral virtue has had enormous influence on all subsequent theories of moral virtue, it should not be

surprising to encounter his influence here, especially in my discussion of the general features of the
theory of moral virtue. Nevertheless, I have tried
hard not to impose Aristotle's thought onto that of
Africans and African Americans. In order to avoid
doing so, I have made every effort to stay within the
thought forms of the latter throughout this study. In
my judgment, any structural similarities between
Aristotle's ethical thought and that of Africans and
African Americans should not be viewed as another
instance of western epistemological imperialism
since the content of the African and African American ethic is decidedly culturally specific.

3. Some African and African American Moral Virtues

1. I am indebted to my colleague William S.
Simpson, who introduced me to C. B. MacPherson's persuasive argument concerning the philo-
sophical basis of the liberal tradition, which gave
rise to the phenomenon he calls possessive individualism. See MacPherson's book, *The Political
Theory of Possessive Individualism: Hobbes to
Locke* (Oxford: Clarendon, 1962).

2. None has studied this phenomenon more
carefully than the West Indian psychiatrist Franz
Fanon. See his books *The Wretched of the Earth*
(New York: Grove, 1963) and *Black Skin, White
Masks* (New York: Grove, 1967).

3. Nelson Mandela, "The ANC and the Govern-
ment Must Meet to Negotiate an Effective Political
Settlement: Letter from Prison to President P. W.
Botha, July 1989," in Greg McCartan, ed., *Nelson
Mandela: Speeches 1990: "Intensify the Struggle*

to Abolish Apartheid" (New York: Pathfinder, 1990), 13.

4. Sylvanus Iniobong Udoidem, "The Epistemological Significance of Proverbs: An African Perspective," in *Presence Africaine,* New Bilingual Series 132 (1984): 134–35.

5. Nelson Mandela was an active participant and leader in the youth league of the ANC; Martin Luther King Jr. was similarly an active member and leader of the Baptist Youth People's Union. Both constituted important training grounds for the two men.

6. Udoidem, "Epistemological Significance," 133.

7. Mandela, "The ANC and the Government," 11–12.

8. David J. Garrow's book, *Bearing the Cross: Martin Luther King, Jr., and the Southern Christian Leadership Conference* (New York: Morrow, 1986), provides the most complete documentation in support of this argument. Another convincing argument in support of this type of syncretism is found in Gabriel Setiloane, "How the Traditional World-View Persists in the Christianity of the Sssotho-Tswana," in Edward Fashole-Luke, Richard Gray, Adrian Hastings, and Godwin Tasie, eds., *Christianity in Independent Africa* (Ibadan, Nigeria: Ibadan University Press, 1978).

4. The Christian Factor in African and African American Social Ethics

1. This position is supported by the work of J. N. K. Mugambi. See his *The African Heritage and Contemporary Christianity* (Kenya: Longman, 1989), 68–69.

2. I am indebted to Lamin O. Sanneh, who has provided a full demonstration of this argument in his important book, *Translating the Message: The Christian Impact on Culture* (Maryknoll, N.Y.: Orbis, 1989).

3. One of the most prominent African American scholars who has pursued this type of scholarly endeavor is Cain Hope Felder. See his *Troubling Biblical Waters: Race, Class, and Family* (Maryknoll, N.Y.: Orbis, 1989), *Race, Racism, and the Biblical Narratives,* Facets (Minneapolis: Fortress Press, 2002), and also the volume he edited, *Stony the Road We Trod: African American Biblical Interpretation* (Minneapolis: Fortress Press, 1991).

4. For a summary description of the role of both of these prophets, see A. Adu Boahen, *African Perspectives on Colonialism* (Baltimore, Md.: Johns Hopkins University Press, 1990), 74–75, 88–89.

5. For one of the best studies of the movement, see Leonard E. Barrett Sr., *The Rastafarians* (Boston: Beacon, 1978).

6. An enormous scholarly literature on these churches was produced in the latter half of the twentieth century. Two of the earliest studies of this phenomenon are B. G. M. Sundler, *Bantu Prophets in South Africa* (London: Oxford University Press, 1961), and H. W. Turner, *History of an African Independent Church: The Church of the Lord (Aladura),* 2 vols. (Oxford: Clarendon, 1967).